HOW TO PICK LOCKS SIMPLIFIED

A DETAILED GUIDE TO BECOME A PRO IN THE ART OF PICKING DIFFERENT KINDS OF LOCKS WITHOUT STRESS

JERRY HUMPHREY

Made with ♥ on the Notion Press Platform
www.notionpress.com

Contents

Title Page

HOW TO PICK LOCKS SIMPLIFIED

A detailed guide to become a pro in the art of picking different kinds of locks without stress

Jerry Humphrey

CHAPTER ONE

INTRODUCTION

It is not rocket science to pick locks, and if you have some basic knowledge, some practice, and a good set of lock picking tools, you can learn how to pick a lock in a short amount of time.

Something you can count on.

As you are about to witness, locks are very stupid creatures that put up very little opposition to people who try to pick them.

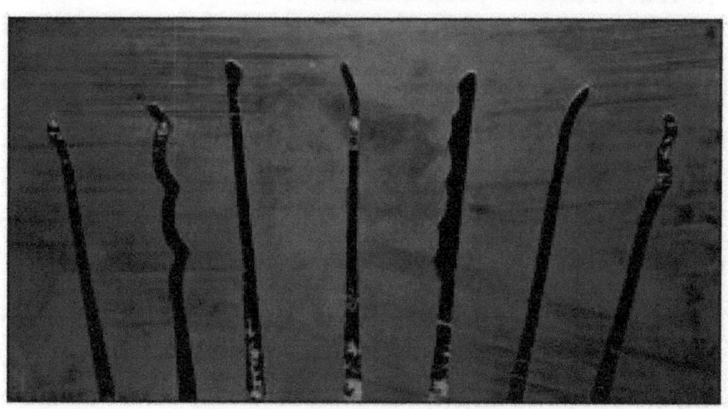

Enter Caption

Thus, let's get started!

What exactly is lock picking?

Lock picking is a method that does not do any damage to the lock when it is used to unlock a lock when there is no key present.

Nonetheless, the goal of each strategy is the same: to imitate the motion of the key in the lock. Single pin picking and raking are two of the lock picking techniques that may be used to achieve this.

Nevertheless, in order to replicate a key, we first need to understand how a key works in a lock.

To achieve this, you must first have an understanding of the operation of the locking mechanism.

There are many different types of locks that are used today, but they all operate on the same fundamental principles; just keep in mind that locks are simple creatures.

For the sake of this piece, we will zero in on the pin tumbler lock, which is both the most basic and the most common kind of lock.

The pin tumbler is the most common kind of locking mechanism and can be found in practically every deadbolt, door lock, and padlock. It accounts for about 90 percent of all locks that are now in use.

They are about 6,000 years old and feature a very simple design for such an antique artifact.

Is Lock Picking Easy?

Also, there is a common misconception that one must possess Zen-level focus in order to learn how to pick a lock.

In order to pick a lock effectively, you will need to spend a significant amount of time sitting still in a room lighted only by candles.

In comparison, the truth is exactly the opposite of what was said.

Lock picking is a skill that can be quickly learned and executed, and it won't take long for you to become proficient in the basic ideas and procedures involved.

If you have a fundamental understanding of lock picking, you will be able to open the great majority of locks that are now in use, even if certain locks are more difficult to pick than others.

An Explanation of How a Pin Tumbler Lock Operates

In order to achieve mastery of the talent of picking locks, we need to have a comprehensive comprehension of the nomenclature and components of the pin tumbler lock.

After we have this knowledge, we will be able to grasp how a lock works and how lock picks may be used to modify a lock!

CHAPTER TWO

What is a lock made of?

The pin tumbler lock consists of six major parts.

Let's briefly examine each of them!

The Cylinder

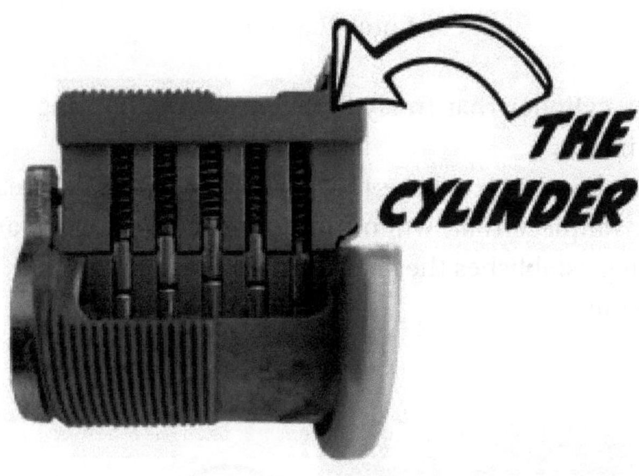

Enter Caption

The lock's cylinder is nothing more than a small container that "houses" the remaining components. Typically, this component is what slips into a door or padlock.

The cylinder forms the top limit of the shear line and is also known as the lock's shell, housing, or body.

The Plug

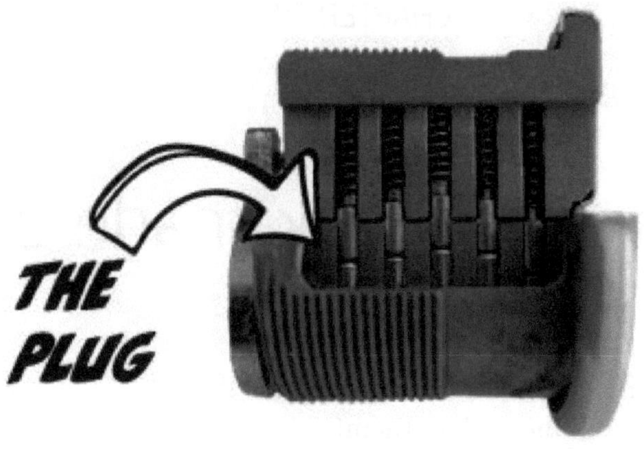

Enter Caption

The plug is a cylinder that freely spins inside the housing to produce a rotating shear line.

The front of the plug is where the key is put, while the rear contains either a cam or tailpiece that, when turned, retracts the latch and unlocks the lock. The plug establishes the shear line's lower limit!

The Shear Line

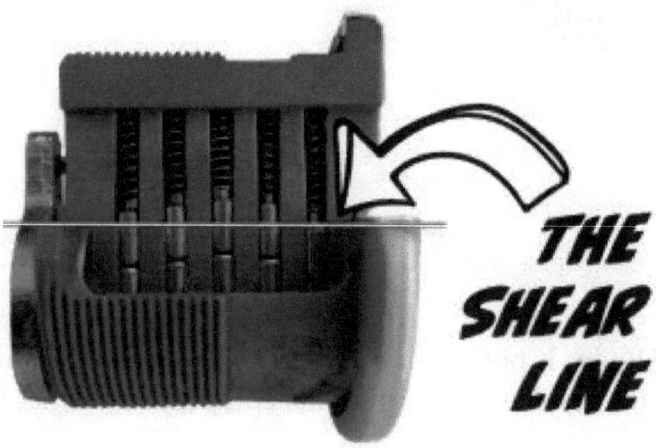

Enter Caption

The shear line is just the space between the cylinder and the spark plug. It is the theoretical axis around which the plug spins inside the housing. If this line is blocked in any manner, the plug and cylinder will get "locked" to each other, preventing the plug from turning.

Once the shear line has been cleaned of any obstacles, the plug will be able to spin freely once again. The shear line is one of the most essential elements to comprehend while picking locks!

Key Pins

Enter Caption

Typically, the pin tumbler lock has two distinct kinds of pins. The lowest set of key pins are responsible for reading the key's cuts. This is accomplished by utilizing pins of various lengths and then cutting a key to match those lengths.

When examining a key, you will observe that there are high and low points. These are referred to as "cuts," and in a minute we'll see how they affect the operation of the lock!

Driver Pins

Enter Caption

The driver pins are the uppermost group of pins with the function of obstructing the shear line.

Essentially, these are the pencil from our simple lock example above! Unlike key pins, driver pins are typically uniform in length.

The Springs

Enter Caption

The last step is the springs, which have two functions. When there is no key in the lock, their initial duty is to press everything into the plug and maintain the driver pins at the shear line. Their second duty is to press the key pins against the keys, which facilitates the reading of the cuts.

Without the springs, the pins might get lodged anywhere in the pin chamber, making it impossible to use a key.

Now that you understand the pin tumbler's fundamental components, let's examine how everything works together to create a completely functional lock!

The following picture depicts the operation of the pin tumbler lock!

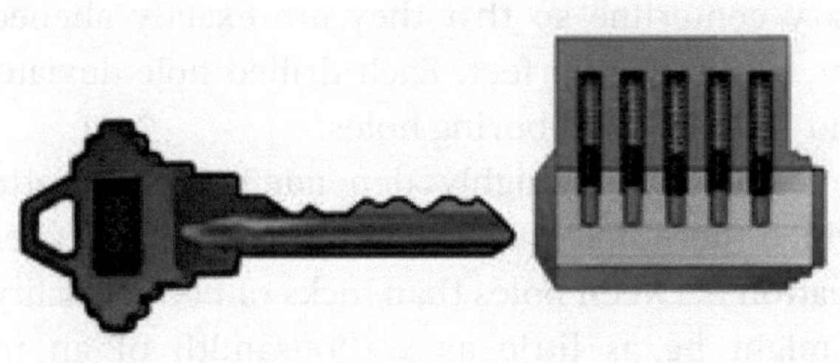

Enter Caption

As can be seen, when the key is inserted into the plug, it causes the key pins to rise. Because the lengths of the key biting and key pins have been matched, the key pins will rise level with the shear line, allowing the driver pins to escape the plug completely.

When the distance between the key pins and driver pins is identical to the shear line, the key may turn the plug to release the lock.

In brief, the key has eliminated all impediments — the pins — from the shear line!

By knowing this procedure, we may begin to comprehend what must be done to pick a lock.

Lock picking is essentially the process of imitating the key by moving the pins to the exact position they would be in if the right key was entered.

But how can we do this? How can we expect to prevent four or five pins from blocking the shear line in the absence of steady key pressure? **How can we prevent them from returning to the plug?**

The response is very awesome!

Why is it possible to pick locks?

Nothing is flawless. Nothing is manufactured without defects or variations from the perfect design. Everything is developed with a focus on tolerance.

None of the locks, pins, or springs are identical. They will constantly differ from one another and from their initial design.

Due to these manufacturing faults, we are able to alter and circumvent locks.

During the manufacturing process, the key pin chambers are drilled along an imaginary centerline so that they are exactly aligned with one another. However, nothing is perfect. Each drilled hole deviates from the real centerline and from its neighboring holes.

The quality of the lock is highly dependent on the attention and precision with which these holes are drilled. In general, cheaper locks will have larger fluctuation between holes than locks of better quality.

This change might be as little as a thousandth of an inch in any circumstance. Nonetheless, it is because to this minute distortion that humans are able to pick locks.

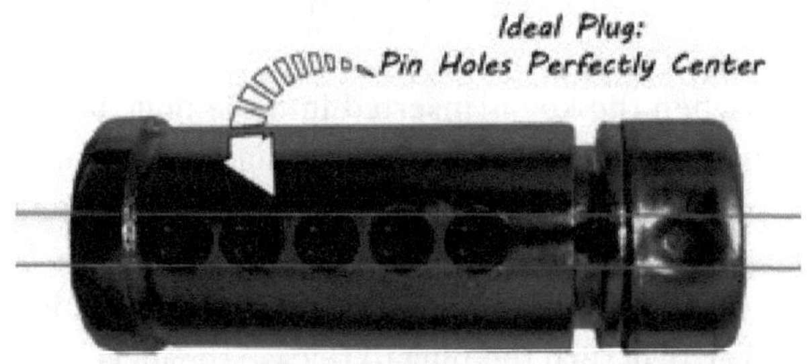

Enter Caption

A flawlessly manufactured lock plug. All chamber holes completely align with the plug's centerline

Exaggerated representation of an actual lock plug. All chamber holes vary in their distance from the plug's real centerline.

However, how can misaligned holes aid in picking locks?

There is a notion that locksmiths or lock pickers refer to as "**binding.**" Imagine inserting a screwdriver into the keyway of a lock and attempting to turn it as if it were a key. However, since the driver pins are still near the shear line, they will prevent the plug from rotating and get entangled between the housing and the plug. This is necessary.

Due to faulty drilling, however, certain pins may bind before others. The first pin to bind and halt the rotation of the plug will be the one that is most off-center in the direction of rotation. This initial pin to bind is referred to as "**the binding pin.**"

Key note: Because perfection is unachievable, the plug's pin chambers are bored slightly off-center. This causes the plug to bind when it is rotated. Due to a binding fault, one pin will bond before to the others and with greater force. The name for this pin is the binding pin.

If necessary, reread this section until you are assured that you fully get the notion of the binding pin. As you will soon learn, the **binding pin** is the actual key to picking locks!

With a grasp of these two fundamental ideas, we can finally take our first practical steps toward learning how to pick a door lock or any other lock.

CHAPTER THREE

Needed Tools for lock picking

Learning how to use the many types of lock picking tools might be one of the most challenging and mind-boggling elements of getting started in this fascinating field.

Yet, in practice, you won't need a lot of gear to get started in lock picking or to enhance your skills.

Even though they have access to hundreds of different tools, even experienced pickers only use a fraction of the options available to them.

There are only three different kinds of tools that may be used to pick a pin-tumbler lock, and they are as follows:

1. Hooks
2. Rakes
3. The Pressure Wrench, often known as the tension Wrench

Let's take a brief glance at each one, and then we'll take a closer look at an excellent beginner kit that has everything you need to get started picking locks!

1. Hooks

Lock picks take the form of hooks, which are slender and pointed implements that allow for pinpoint accuracy when used inside a lock.

Due to their pinpoint precision, they are ideal selecting tools for single pin picking, a kind of pin picking in which players must locate and remove a single pin at a time.

Enter Caption

Hooks are available in a wide range of sizes and shapes.

Everyone is responsible for the same task, which consists of moving the individual pins one at a time.

The typical short hook, which may be seen above, is the best option for the initial hook.

2. Rakes

Rakes are basically the opposite of hooks in their function.

They are designed with a plethora of humps and bumps that allow them to manage the most number of pins in the shortest amount of time feasible.

This makes them ideal for raking, a method that involves rapidly and arbitrarily drawing them over several pins at the same time in order to set multiple pins at the same time.

Enter Caption

Rakes may be broken down into a few distinct categories, much like hooks.

Yet, they all perform the same goal, which is manipulating several pins concurrently.

As was just shown, the Bogota is the perfect rake for those just starting out.

3. Adjusting the tension on the tools and equipment

Interestingly, the most important tool for picking locks is one that only a select few individuals who are not themselves lock pickers are familiar with.

The rotating device, often known as the tension wrench, is its common name.

To provide torque to the plug and ensure that the pins are in place, the tensioning device is used.

It is not feasible to pick a lock without this particular device.

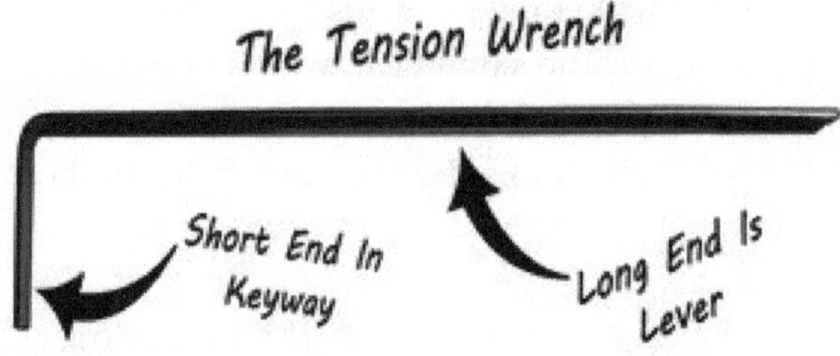

Enter Caption

Beginner Lock Pick Set

I would recommend the GSP Ghost Pick Set to you if you are looking to purchase your very first set of lock picking equipment.

All of the tensioning tools and lock picks are made out of stainless steel of grade 420, which is suitable for surgical use.

Molded plastic grips are also included on the lock picks. These grips prevent the picks from poking your fingers while you are using them.

If the GSP Ghost lock pick set doesn't capture your interest, I highly suggest that you look for another set that has a configuration that is similar to that of the GSP Ghost set!

Before we go any further, I would like to make it clear that it is much better to obtain a small number of lock picks of a superior quality than a significant number of lock picks of a lower grade.

Make an investment in quality and stay away from the lock picking tools on Amazon!

If the lock that you are trying to pick has a keyway that is completely open, you may swiftly get out of there by using bobby pins or paperclips.

Think about consulting the guides that come after this one for similar methods!

Now that you have the necessary tools, it's time to get your hands dirty and start picking locks!

CHAPTER FOUR

Using a Wrench to Release Stress

Now is the time to become an expert with your first tool, which is the tension wrench.

This little animal is responsible for two very important tasks, namely:

In the first place, it gives the user the required leverage to spin the plug and set up a binding pin.

Always keep in mind that the binding pin is necessary in order to pick locks.

Second, it acts as a key in that it maintains the position of the pins you elevate with your pick over the shear line.

This is how it should be done

To start, you will need to position the tension wrench so that it is positioned at the bottom of the keyway. Then, you will need to apply a very little amount of force in the direction that the key would normally spin in order to unlock the lock, which is often counterclockwise.

Another example of what I mean by "light force" is the amount of pressure needed to depress a key on a standard computer keyboard.

It is really easy to carry.

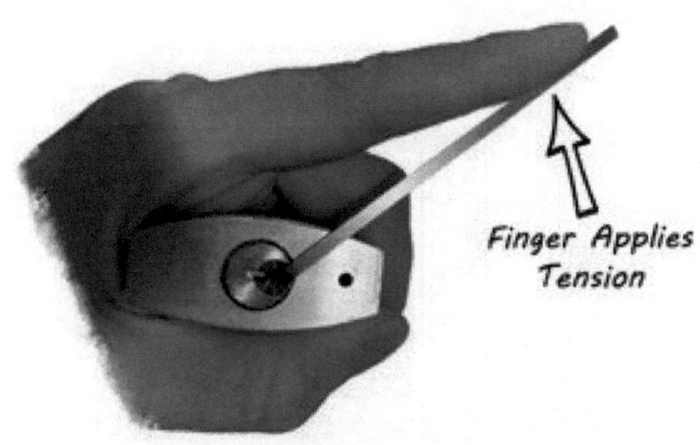

Enter Caption

In most cases, this moderate amount of force or tension is all that is required to produce a binding pin.

You will now comprehend the need of the binding pin after reading this!

If you use a pick to lift the binding pin to the shear line or to the height that the right key would lift it to, the bind will be broken, and the plug will continue to revolve until it binds on the next binding pin. This can be accomplished by either using the shear line or the height that the right key would lift it to.

But, an incredibly wonderful event takes place as well!

As the driver pin hits the shear line, the plug makes a small ledge for the driver pin to rest on because it rotates ever-so-slightly as it approaches the shear line.

The process of doing this is called "setting a pin," and as a result, the driver pin stays above the shear line and outside the plug!

Check out the image below below to get a clearer sense of how to insert a pin.

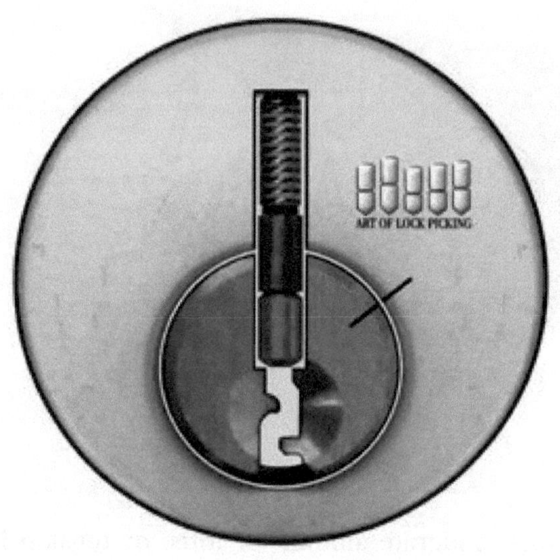

Enter Caption

Let's get down to business now that we are aware of the goal that is contained behind the lock on the door.

Put the end of your tension wrench that is shorter into the hole at the bottom of the keyhole.

Although if this is not always necessary, there are times when we have to choose which side of the lock unlocks first.

To do this, first crank the tension wrench in a clockwise direction, and then turn it in the opposite direction while applying pressure.

Before coming to a complete halt, the plug has to be turned very slowly in both directions.

As you turn the plug in both directions, you need to keep a careful eye on the tension wrench as it stops at each position.

If it looks hard and lacks suppleness, the direction of rotation that you are now going in is probably not proper.

Alternately, the direction of rotation that should be used will have a softer feel and more give to it.

When the plug is turned, most low-cost locks, including the great majority of padlocks, may be opened in any way. This is an additional factor to take into account.

After it has been established in which direction the plug will rotate, the wrench may then be tightened in that particular direction.

In order to pick the lock successfully, the amount of force that is used is essential.

When an excessive amount of force is applied, the pins will get jammed beneath the shear line.

In the event that inadequate strain is exerted, the pins will simply revert to their original position inside the plug.

Learning to have a good "feel" for the tension wrench is the single most crucial step in the process of picking a lock.

While using the tension wrench, it is best to begin with the lightest touch possible and then gradually add pressure as necessary. This is a good rule of thumb to follow.

The binding pin will start to bind as soon as there is even a little amount of force applied to the plug.

The next thing you need to do is find this pin and then push it over the shear line.

Let us now go to the first way of lock picking that we will become proficient in.

CHAPTER FIVE

How to Open a Lock With a Single Pin

Now we finally have a handle on all of this terminology, we can turn our attention to the issue at hand, which is picking a lock.

First, we'll have a look at the lock picking method known as single pin picking, sometimes referred to as SPP for short. This method is only one of many fundamental approaches that may be used to pick a lock.

With this method, we elevate each pin one at a time by hand using a lock pick that is shaped like a hook.

Despite the fact that picking locks with a single pin is neither the fastest nor the easiest approach, it is the best method for learning how to pick a padlock or door lock since it provides us with a better understanding of what is occurring inside a lock.

It's possible that having this information will be the deciding factor in whether or not you achieve mastery.

After all of that, I say we try our hand at it.

1st step: At the first phase, tension is applied in order to produce the first binding pin.

It is important to keep in mind that in order to successfully set pins at the shear line and select a lock, you will first need to manufacture your first binding pin by applying a little amount of rotational pressure to the plug.

In order to do this, insert the shorter end of your tension wrench into the bottom of the keyway, and then apply very little tension on the plug.

During the whole process of picking a lock, make sure that your tension wrench is under this amount of tension.

2. Identify the position of the first binding pin

When you have created your first binding pin, the next step is to find its location.

After that...

The binding pin will be subjected to a larger "binding" force than the other pins, and as a result, it will be more stiff and challenging to lift than the non-binding pins.

You are, in essence, looking for a pin that is not wobbly in its position!

Put a pick with a hook-like prong into the keyway, then work your way all the way to the back of the lock until you find the pin at the very end.

To begin, raise each pin one at a time and observe how it feels in your hand.

Repeat the process of exploring each pin until you find the one that has a distinct sensation and is more difficult to move.

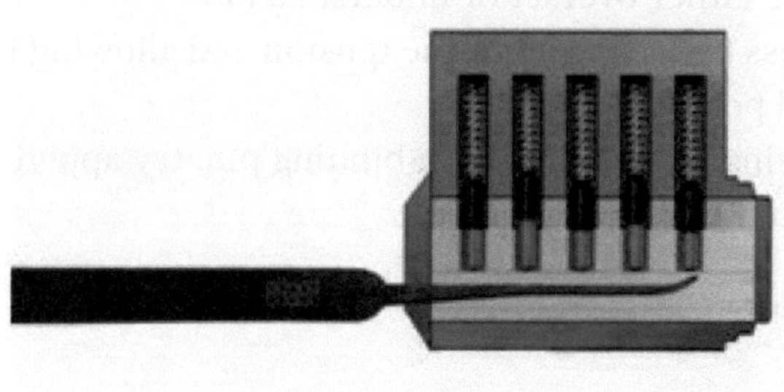

Enter Caption

Third Step: Lift and place the first binding pin in its location.

Since the first binding pin has been found, the next step is to put it in place.

Raise the binding pin until you can feel or hear the plug rotating slightly or clicking loudly, whichever comes first.

In most cases, the presence of either of these two signals indicates that a driver pin has been properly set!

4. Determine the location of the second binding pin and install it

You have located and adjusted the first pin that the lock is binding on; however, the lock is now binding on a different pin.

Continue the procedure of lifting each pin with care until you come across another one that is rigid and difficult to move.

Like you did before, continue to gently raise the pin until you feel or hear a definite click on the plug. This will indicate that the plug has begun to spin slightly.

Step five: Carry out the procedure of finding and inserting binding pins once again

Maintain your search for the binding pins and bring them up to the shear line as you go.

When all of the pins are in their correct positions, the shear line will no longer be blocked, the plug will spin all the way around, and the lock will be unlocked!

You just choose your first lock, congratulations!

Note: In the event that you are unable to discover a binding pin, it is possible that you have either overset or underset a pin.

Resume the process by letting go of the tension and allowing the pins to fall into their original position.

If you are still having trouble finding a binding pin, try applying slightly additional pressure to the plug.

CHAPTER SIX

Guide to using a rake to pick lock

Lock picking may be accomplished with relative ease using the raking method.

Raking is an extremely powerful and extreme form of the picking method, and its primary purpose is to knock as many pins as possible down to the shear line in the shortest amount of time.

When trying to break locks that include additional security measures such as security pins and sidebars, it becomes nearly completely ineffective, despite the fact that it may be a lot of fun and is a pretty speedy method for defeating many basic locks.

There are several subtypes of rakes to choose from.

Scrubbing is the method that we are going to talk about; in essence, it is the same motion as when we clean our teeth!

Initially, apply strain to make a binding pin by following these steps:

1st step: The first thing that has to be done is to remake the binding pin.

Put the short end of your tension wrench into the bottom of the keyway, and then rotate the plug slowly and gently!

Second step: is to insert the lock pick, and then proceed to the next step

Scrub the Pins Then, insert your rake into the keyway, push it all the way to the back of the lock, and gently draw upward so that your pick lifts the pins just a little bit.

You should start by scrubbing the pins with a good amount of velocity, much as you would the tops of your teeth if you were brushing them.

Alter the angle, height, and speed at which you move your pick as you work.

After ten seconds, if the lock is still not open, the tension on the lock has to be removed so that it may be reset and the process can start again.

Before successfully breaking a lock, it is common practice to have to reset the lock a number of times first.

Keep cleaning those pins until the plug turns completely and the lock may be opened!

If you are still unable to scrape your lock, try using a little more or a little less force than you did before.

Raking is really more about exerting the appropriate amount of tension than it is about having the ability to pick locks.

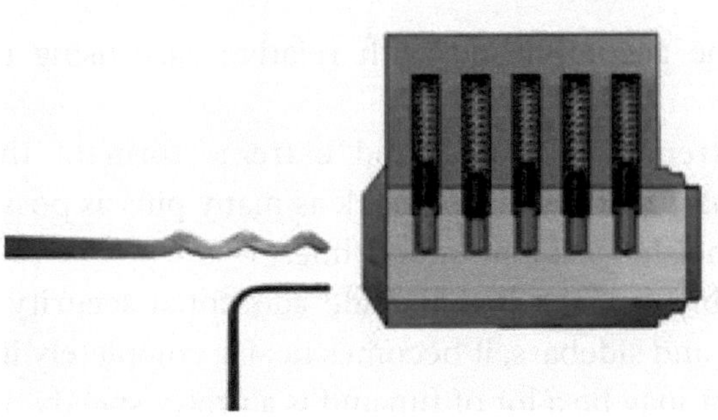

Enter Caption

Notice crucial:

As you're raking, keep an eye on your stress levels.

While choosing single pins, a larger level of stress may sometimes be tolerated; but, when raking, an excessive amount of strain can cause a pick to break.

The Legality of Picking Locks

The ability to pick locks is not the primary challenge that those who are interested in the activity face; rather, the difficulty comes from the fact that the activity is prohibited.

The act of picking locks is looked down upon quite poorly by the majority of people in today's society.

As a result of this bias, a great number of people believe that it should be against the law to own lock picks.

In point of fact, as long as you have the permission of the person whose lock you are trying to pick, it is legal to own a set of lock picks and to use them in the majority of states and countries throughout the world.

Residents of the United States may use an interactive version of the map below to learn more about the legal restrictions placed on picking locks in the country.

Move your mouse pointer over the map of the United States to determine whether or not it is legal to possess lock picks in your state, and then click on the state to read relevant legal sections.

In addition to that, make sure that you read our brand-new, in-depth article on the legal implications of picking locks.

It is not very long and reading it is something that you should do.

Being familiar with the law is your best line of defense in the event that you find yourself in trouble with the authorities.

Keep safe!

CHAPTER SEVEN

Six Easy Steps to picking locks

It's quite likely that you've misplaced your house key at some point in your life, regardless of whether or not you're willing to confess it.

It's possible that you forgot them at a friend's home, in which case you wouldn't feel safe leaving a spare key in the front yard.

After that...

The ability to pick a lock might be valuable in a variety of situations. [Clarification needed]

Six Simple Steps That Will Teach You How to Pick Your First Lock

You will be able to pick locks as easily as if you've been doing it all your life if you follow these instructions carefully.

My experience in picking locks spans over a decade at this point.

And he has madc thc dccision to share this knowledge and this enthusiasm with each and every one of us.

Lock picking is a skill that will come in useful in the event that the world completely collapses and our natural impulses to survive are triggered.

What precisely is meant by the term "lock picking"?

There are a few different technical explanations for picking locks, but none of them do a good job of explaining the activity to someone who is just starting out.

Thus, let's explain it in terms that a layperson may understand.

The art of lock picking consists of deceiving a lock into believing that the correct key has been used to open it.

Locks are very simple and thoughtless entities, each having a single, predetermined path for how they are operated.

Because of its straightforward nature, picking locks is a skill that almost anybody who wishes to do so can easily acquire and put into practice.

But, in order to acquire this capacity, we will first need to have a basic understanding of the workings of a key in order to be able to replicate it.

How does a Key function

In the interest of this guide, we will analyze the pin tumbler lock, which is both the simplest and most common kind of lock now in circulation.

This particular kind of lock has been in use for over 6,000 years, and its origins may be traced all the way back to ancient Egypt.

Since this mechanism is present in more than 90 percent of the locks in the world, it is the most likely candidate for our efforts to circumvent the security system.

Therefore, let's have a look at how they run their business.

The conventional pin tumbler lock is comprised of the following six components:

• Housing: This component of the lock is often fastened to a door or padlock and contains all of the components that make the lock operational.

• Plug: In contrast to the housing, the plug is a cylinder, and after the correct key has been entered, it is able to spin freely.

• Shear Line: The shear line, which is colored green, is the component that is most important for picking a lock.

It refers to the actual distance that separates the housing and the plug in question.

• Springs: The springs are there to force the pins into the plug, which is the function of the springs.

• Driver Pins: The driver pins, which are blue in color, are what make it possible for a lock to latch and stay locked.

The driver pins will often be situated in the middle of the gap between the housing and the plug in the event that the correct key is not placed into the plug.

Because of this, a binding is created, which stops the connection from spinning all the way and thus locks the device.

• Important Pins:

The top of a key will come into contact with the plug's red key pins when the key is inserted into the plug.

The pattern of each key has a certain length that correlates with the length of the key pin that goes with it.

When the appropriate key is inserted, the key pins are all brought to a level where they are flush with the shear line.

In addition, the driver pins are pushed out of the plug in such a way that they maintain a flush alignment with the shear line.

When the distance between the key pins and the driver pins exactly matches that of the shear line, the lock may be released by twisting the key. This occurs when the shear line is parallel to the key pins and the driver pins.

As can be seen, the point of picking a lock is to manipulate the pins in such a way that they are no longer able to stop the plug from rotating in the same way that a key would.

Let's now go on to some more conventional locksmithing work, shall we?

Tools and equipment essential to the art of lock picking

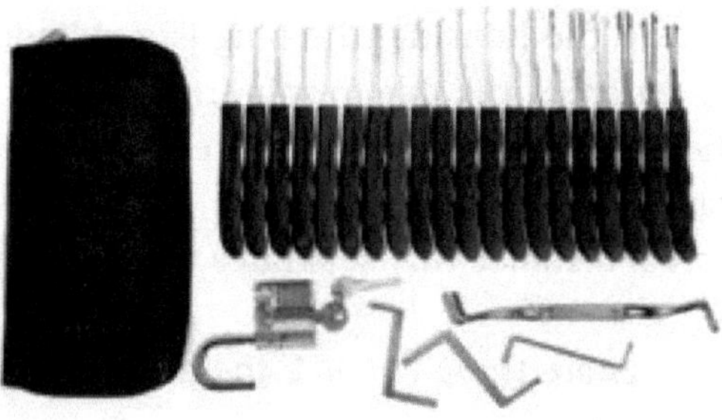

Enter Caption

You are going to want a lock pick as well as a torque wrench.

The purpose of the lock pick is to move the pins closer to the shear line so that the lock may be picked.

It should come as no surprise that there is a multitude of pick kinds, each of which requires a different strategy.

Because this is a tutorial for novices, we will concentrate on raking, which is the method of lock picking that is both the quickest and easiest to perform.

For this strategy, a lock pick of the "rake" kind is required.

Out of the many different kinds of rake picks that are available, the snake rake is the one that is used the most.

These picks have a long and jagged tip that, much like a key, can operate many pins at the same time.

In addition to the pick, there is another instrument known as a torque wrench that plays a very important role.

This "L"-shaped wrench serves two important purposes simultaneously.

To begin, it provides the leverage required to turn the plug, functioning in much the same way that a key would.

Second, and most importantly, it supplies the necessary torque to position and keep the pins at the shear line when we pick them. This is a very important function.

If this force wasn't applied, the pins would easily slide back into the plug, making it impossible to unlock the lock under any circumstance.

you can easily get this complete lock picking set online, which has a see-through padlock that may be used for training purposes.

Verify the rules in your area since certain places do not allow citizens to possess tools used for picking locks.

If you live in the United States, you should check out this quick and dirty guide to the rules of lock picking.

Bobby pins can be used as lock picks to open standard pin tumbler locks, so all you MacGyvers out there, don't feel bad if you've never heard of this trick before.

How to pick Your First Lock in Six Steps

Let's move on to the topic that you came here to learn about now that we have a fundamental understanding of pin tumbler locks and the tools required to pick them.

The process of picking a lock may be broken down into six simple phases, which are shown here.

• The first step is to place the end of the tension wrench that is shorter into the bottom of the keyway on the lock.

Put just the slightest amount of pressure possible with one or two fingers to the wrench in the direction that you would generally turn the key (typically clockwise).

* Be sure that you keep this amount of torque applied to the wrench throughout the rest of the phases.

Importantly, understanding just how much pressure to apply is what differentiates someone who is just starting out from someone who is an expert.

The ability to maintain tension is the single most important talent, and it can only be obtained by consistent practice.

• The second step is to insert the rake pick into the keyway of the lock and then move it all the way to the back of the lock while continuing to apply very little pressure to the wrench.

• The third step is to scrape lightly with a gentle motion while pulling the pick out while applying upward pressure to the pins with the rake's end.

On your way out, you need to be sure you bump all of the pins.

• The fourth step is to ensure that adequate force has been applied, at which point a number of the lock's pins should have settled at the shear line and the plug should have twisted somewhat.

Be aware, however, that this change in emphasis to the newcomer will, for the most part, go undetected.

• The fifth step is to re-introduce the pick into the back of the lock and to proceed with the scraping action on the pins once again.

Continue carrying out these steps until all of the pins have been positioned.

If, after five or six tries, the lock still will not open, release some of the tension on the wrench and pay close attention to hear when the pins drop into place.

If you do not hear a drop, this is a clear sign that you have used an excessive amount of force while using the torque wrench.

Repeat the process by changing the amount of pressure you apply to the wrench and rake the pins once more.

• The sixth step involves determining the required tension and then setting all of the pins. At this point, the plug will give and allow full rotation with the torque wrench, just as it would have done so if the appropriate key had been used.

The first of your locks has been picked without incident.

Now, you should not use these methods on homes in the neighborhood since it is considered to be burglary.

This is considered a minor infraction.

CHAPTER EIGHT

Simple Guide to Bobby Pin Lock picking

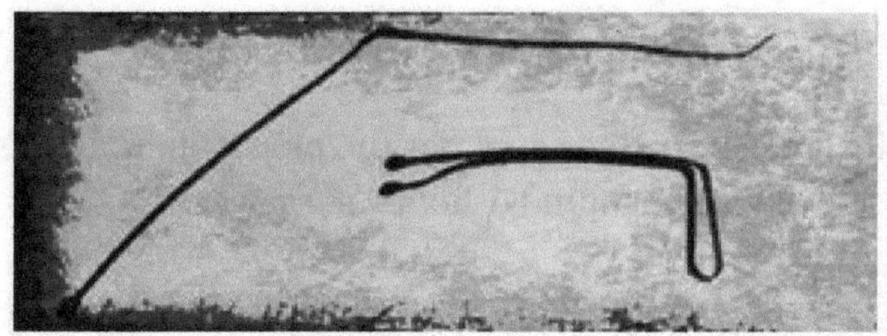

Enter Caption

Using bobby pins to pick locks provides a peculiar sense of accomplishment.

A satisfaction accompanied with a degree of confidence that shouts to the sky, "I am the lord of my fate; let no door, padlock, or other similar obstructions stand in my way, because I am a lock picker, master of pins, and security destroyer!"

If you too would want to learn how to pick a lock with a bobby pin and shout these words into the night, then this instruction is for you.

For simplicity and organization, this guide is divided into three sections:

How a Simple Lock Operates

Locks are incredibly basic animals that, in reality, provide little protection against people who understand how they function.

Before we can get into the actual lock-picking tactics, we must first grasp what we are attempting to achieve inside the lock - don't worry, this will be brief!

While there are several different kinds of locks, this tutorial will concentrate on the pin tumbler lock mechanism, which accounts for almost 90 percent of locks in use today. This indicates that if you master picking these locks, you have a decent probability of picking the majority of locks available.

The Tumbler Pin

The basic pin and tumbler lock consists of six primary components: the plug, driver pins, key pins, springs, the shear line, and a casing to keep everything in place. While each component plays a significant role, we shall focus primarily on the "shear line."

Through the pins, the shear line separates the plug from the housing and is the reason why a lock will not spin without the right key.

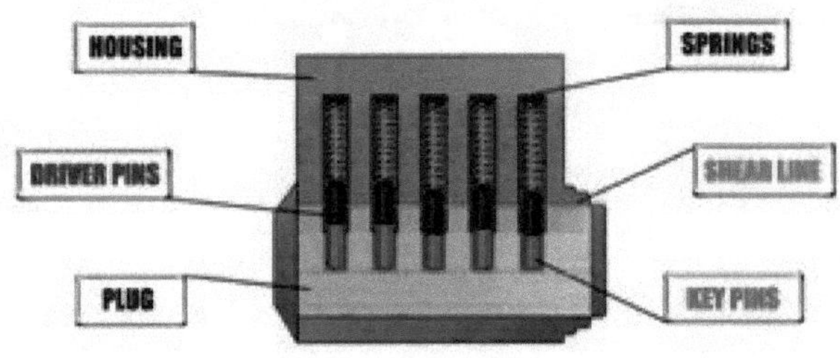

Enter Caption

When the right key is inserted into the lock, the key pins are lifted level with the shear line, forcing the driver pins out of the plug.

When the difference between the key pins and driver pins is identical to the shear line, the plug may be rotated to unlock the device. This is best shown by the picture that follows.

Therefore, the purpose of lock picking is to imitate the key by pressing the pins flat with the shear line, so enabling us to spin and release the lock.

However, how can we prevent the pins from slipping back into the plug after they have been lifted?

Here is when things become interesting.

The Plug: Manufacture Defects

The basic truth is that nothing can ever be made flawlessly. During the manufacturing process of a lock, an acceptable error tolerance is permitted. These flaws in the lock make it possible for us to pick them.

Let's examine a common vulnerability that makes lock picking feasible.

Holes are bored during the manufacture of the plug to accommodate the pins. These holes would be perfectly aligned with the real centerline of the plug in a flawless plug. However, since nothing can ever be manufactured to perfectly, there will always be variance in the actual location of these holes.

This discrepancy may be as little as a thousandth of an inch, and it is because to this minute deviation that humans are able to pick locks.

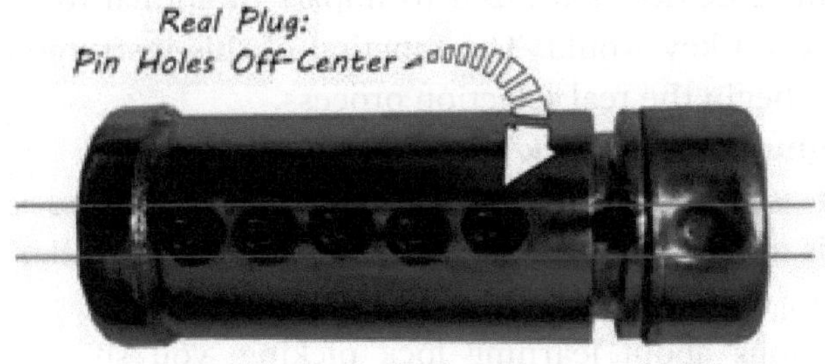

Enter Caption

So why is this essential? As can be seen, each pin is located at a different distance from the plug's real centerline.

This indicates that when rotational strain is applied to the plug, one pin will bind first between the housing and the plug. This pin is referred to as the "binding pin" by lock pickers and is defined as the pin farthest from the plug's real centerline.

We should now be familiar with two essential notions.

1. To disengage a lock, we must first raise all of its pins to the shear line.

2. Due to manufacturing defects, pins will bind in a specified sequence, beginning with the pin farthest from the real center-line of the plug.

Now that we have an understanding of these two fundamental notions, it is time to create our tools and start picking locks.

2. Creating Bobby Pin Lock Picks

If you've ever seen a movie in which a superspy picks a lock, you may have noticed that they often insert one tool into the lock and jiggle it until the lock opens.

Lock picking is straightforward and can be accomplished fast on simple locks, however the movies do not do it credit.

Two tools are required to pick a lock: a pick (obviously) and a tension wrench.

The pick enables us to elevate the pins to the shear line, exactly like the key does. Using a bobby pin, you may create a number of various forms of lock picks; however, this lesson will concentrate on the hook style pick.

This bizarre little device is utilized to impart rotational torque to the lock, similar to how a key would. The function of this instrument will be revealed when we begin the real selection process.

A Quality Beginning Lock Pick Set

Lock picking with a hairpin might be a pleasant endeavor, but unfortunately it is not always successful. Some locks have smaller keyways that are too narrow for a bobby pin to fit through.

If you are serious about learning lock picking, you should strongly consider purchasing a basic lock picking kit.

The GSP Ghost Lock Pick Set is one of the finest lock pick sets for beginners. This high-quality lock pick kit has everything a novice needs to get started in the craft of lock picking.

Continue reading if you prefer to go MacGyver-style, though.

Therefore, now that we know what we need, let's begin bending bobby pins!

CHAPTER NINE

Pick for Bobby Pin Lock

Creating our bobby pin lock pick is a quick and easy process.

Initially, we must remove the rounded tip from the straight side of the bobby pin. This may be readily achieved using fingernails, pliers, or even teeth.

Once the rubber end is removed, we may begin bending the pipe. Begin by separating the bobby pin and generally straightening it.

Then, insert the straight end of the hairpin about one centimeter, or about one-third of an inch, into the keyhole of the lock and apply sufficient pressure to bend the straight end into a hook. The outcome should like this in appearance.

Now that the lock pick is complete, let's move on to forging the tension wrench.

Tension Wrench with Bobby Pin

The tension wrench has a straightforward "L" design, making its formation as easy as a single bend. Start by inserting the closed end of the bobby pin approximately an inch into the keyhole of the lock and applying downward pressure until the pin is bent 90 degrees. That concludes the discussion.

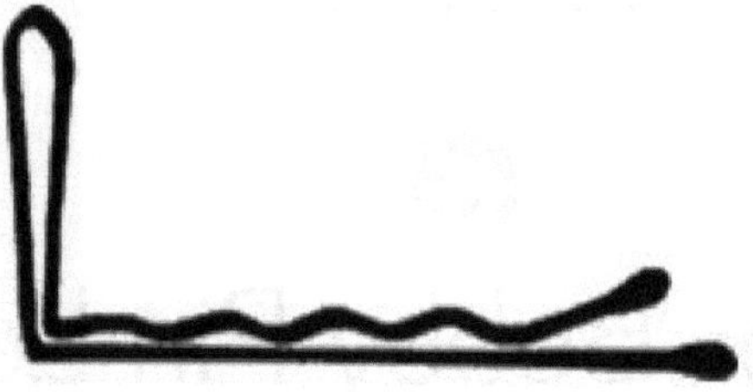

Enter Caption

Now that we have a functional set of lock picking tools, it is essential to understand how a pin and tumbler locking mechanism works before attempting to pick any locks.

Now that we own picks and a tension wrench, we can get filthy!

3. How to Open a Lock Using a Bobby Pin

Before we can play with our new toys, we must first learn how to use the bobby pin tension wrench correctly. As was briefly described previously, this little device serves two purposes.

First, it provides the leverage necessary to provide rotational stress to the plug, analogous to a key. Second, this little piece of bent metal assists us in keeping the pins at the shear line when we select them. What then? Well, let's have a peek.

Keeping in mind the notion of the binding pin, when rotational strain is applied to the plug, the binding pin will... bind and prevent the plug from spinning. Using our pick, we push the pin to the shear line while it is bound. Here, everything is brought together.

As the first binding pin hits the shear line, the plug will rotate ever-so-slightly as it seeks to bind on the next pin farthest from the real centerline. However, something else unusual occurs.

Because the plug spins somewhat, the pin we pushed up will settle on top of the plug, and it will remain there as long as you maintain the proper tension. This is referred to as "setting a pin," as seen below.

Utilizing a Tension Wrench

Now is the moment! Now that we know precisely what our objective is within the lock, we can begin picking those bothersome pins.

First, place the shorter, closed end of our bobby pin tension wrench into the bottom portion of the keyhole and apply little tension in the direction the key would spin.

The amount of strain we apply is crucial (no pun intended) to our success or failure in picking a lock.

If we use excessive force, we risk binding more than the initial binding pin, which makes it impossible to discern the binding sequence and set the other pins. However, if insufficient force is used, the pin will not be seated and will fall back into the plug.

A typical rule of thumb for utilizing the tension wrench is to begin with little tension and gradually increase it as required.

The primary distinction between a beginner and a master is the ability to intuitively use a tension wrench.

Now that there is a little amount of strain on the plug, we must find the first binding pin and set it with our newly fashioned bobby pin lock pick.

CHAPTER TEN

Picking/Unlocking a Lock

Now, the time for which we have all been waiting, let's begin choosing pins. While there are other lock picking techniques and kinds of lock picks, we will concentrate on what is known as "single pin picking" using our "hook-type" bobby pin lock pick.

Insert our bobby pin tension wrench into the lock once again and apply the required force to bind the initial binding pin. Throughout the entire process of picking and setting pins, it is necessary to maintain tension on the plug.

Once the plug is secured, the bobby pin lock pick may be inserted into the lock with the little hook facing the pins. Beginning at the rear, probe each pin by pulling it up slightly to determine its liftability.

With the exception of the binding pin, the majority of pins should be reasonably simple to raise. However, the binding pin will feel firmer and more difficult to move.

After locating the first binding pin via investigation, it is time to move it out of the way. Using our pick, apply upward pressure on the pin; when it hits the shear line, the plug will rotate slightly as the pin sets.

It is also normal to detect a tiny vibration via the tension wrench; however, because we are using bobby pins, it is doubtful that we would experience this phenomenon. Keep in mind that we just removed the driver pin from the plug, so do not be frightened if you feel the key pin jiggling within the plug. Everything is good.

Now that the first binding pin has been set, we must identify and set the second binding pin. As in the past, we must continue exploring the other pins until we locate the stubborn one. Once located, we may shove it toward the shear line to place the second pin.

The whole process of picking a lock consists of repeatedly finding and setting the binding pin. As soon as all the pins are in place, the plug will spin entirely as if we had a key, and the lock will disengage. If the above occurs, Congratulations! You have successfully picked your first lock!

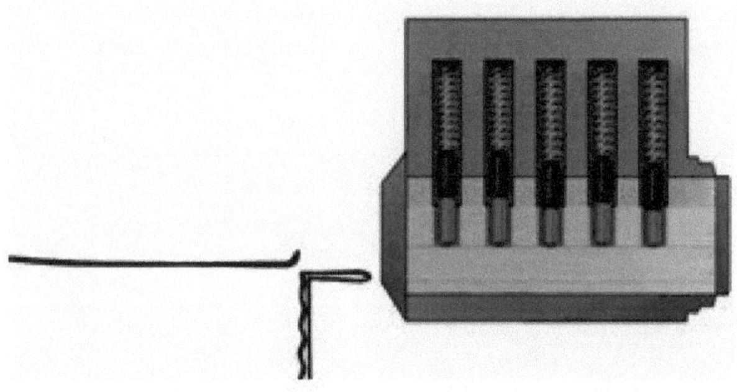

Enter Caption

Note that if you have trouble setting pins, meaning that they do not set or continue to fall, you will likely need to modify the amount of force you are providing to the tension wrench. Remember that the tension of the tension wrench is essential to picking any lock.

In conclusion

To end this instruction on bobby pin lock picking, I would want to discuss two matters.

The first is that you should never use these talents maliciously and should only use them on your own locks or with the lock owner's consent.

Second, about your locks; it is strongly recommended that you avoid practicing on locks that you rely on, such as the deadbolt on your front door. This could cause permanent damage to them. It is advised that you purchase or salvage practice locks for the purpose of training.

In addition, if you enjoy this hobby while using bobby pins or paperclips to pick locks, you should consider purchasing a real set of lock picks. They are a very inexpensive investment, and having the proper equipment can greatly boost your success at picking locks and honing your abilities.

If you appreciated this little instruction, best of luck whenever you go picking!

The End

9 798889 864097

Printed by Libri Plureos GmbH in Hamburg,
Germany